Orchot Chaim

L'HaRosh

With

Iggeret Ha'Ramban
&
Iggeret Ha'Gra

SimchatChaim.com

There is no known book without mistakes. Therefore, I ask in every language of application if anyone has any questions, comments, clarifications, corrections, please send to:
<u>simchatchaim@yahoo.com</u>

All material used in this section may not be used for commercial purposes, but only for study and teaching.

To get this book or books and information Email me at:
<u>simchatchaim@yahoo.com</u>

Copyright©All Rights Reserved to

<u>www.simchatchaim.com</u>

All rights reserved to the Editor©Itzhak Hoki Aboudi

Second edition 2024

Orchot Chaim — Book Contents

The contents of the book

Page	Chapter
3.	Biography of the HaRosh
11.	Chapter 1 for Sunday
19.	Chapter 2 for Monday
27.	Chapter 3 for Tuesday
33.	Chapter 4 for Wednesday
41.	Chapter 5 for Thursday
49.	Chapter 6 for Friday

Orchot Chaim   Book Contents

55.   Chapter 7
                for Saturday

61.   Iggeret Ha'Ramban

69.   Iggeret Ha'Gra

Orchot Chaim   The Ha'Rosh

Biography of the Ha'Rosh

Rabbi Asher ben Yechiel [Hebrew: אשר בן יחיאל, or Asher ben Yechiel, sometimes Asheri] [Born 1250 or 1259 – Deceased 1327] was an eminent rabbi and Talmudist best known for his abstract of Talmudic law. He is often referred to as **Rabbenu Asher** - Our Rabbi Asher. Or by the Hebrew acronym for this title, the Rosh [רא"ש]. His yahrzeit is on 9 Cheshvan.

Biography

The **Rosh** was probably born in Cologne, Holy Roman Empire, and deceased in Toledo. His family was prominent for learning and piety, his father Yechiel was a Talmudist, and one of his ancestors was Rabbi Eliezer ben Nathan [the Ra'aban]. Asher had eight sons, the most prominent

Orchot Chaim — The Ha'Rosh

of whom were Yaakov [author of the Arba'ah Turim] and Yehuda.

In 1286, King Rudolf I had instituted a new persecution of the Jews, and the great teacher of the **Rosh**, Rabbi Meir of Rothenburg, left Germany but was captured and imprisoned. The Rosh raised a ransom for his release, but Rabbi Meir refused it, for fear of encouraging the imprisonment of other rabbis. Thereafter the Rosh assumed Rabbi Meir's position in Worms. He was, however, forced to emigrate [in all likelihood, a victim of blackmail by the government, aimed at acquiring his fortune]. After leaving Germany, he first settled in southern France, and then in Toledo, Spain, where he became rabbi on the recommendation of Rabbi Solomon ben Abraham Aderet [Ra'shba]. Rabbenu Asher's son Yehuda testified to the fact that he died in poverty.

Orchot Chaim — The Ha'Rosh

Rabbeinu Asher deceased in Toledo on 9 Cheshvan 5088 [1327 CE]. His known surviving children were said to have been killed in the ensuing persecutions that affected Spain in 1392.

Rabbenu Asher possessed **methodical and systematic** Talmudic knowledge, and was distinguished for his ability to analyze and thereby clarify long Talmudic discussions. The Rosh was known for his independent legal reasoning - We must not be guided in our decisions by the admiration of great men, and in the event of a law not being clearly stated in the Talmud, we are not bound to accept it, even if it be based on the works of the Geonim. [For instance, the Rosh ruled that the liturgy of the Geonim was not subject to the Talmudic rule against change in the prayers.]

Orchot Chaim   The Ha'Rosh

Rabbenu Asher was opposed to the study of secular knowledge, especially philosophy. He held that philosophy is based on critical research, whereas religion is based on tradition and the two are thus **incapable of harmonization**. He said that **none that go unto her may return** - in fact, he thanked God for having saved him from its influence, and boasted of possessing no knowledge outside the Torah. He attempted to issue a decree against the study of non-Jewish learning. One effect of this attitude was to limit his influence on secular Spanish Jewry. At the same time, within rabbinic circles, "he transplanted the strict and narrow Talmudic spirit from Germany to Spain", and this, in some measure, turned Spanish Jews from secular research to the study of the Talmud.

Orchot Chaim — The Ha'Rosh

Rabbenu Asher Works

Rabbenu Asher's best-known work is his abstract of Talmudic law. This work specifies the final, practical halakha, leaving out the intermediate discussion and concisely stating the final decision. It omits areas of law limited to Eretz Yisrael [such as agricultural and sacrificial laws] as well as the **Aggadic** portions of the Talmud.

Rabbi Asher's son Yaakov compiled a list of the decisions found in the work, under the title **Piskei Ha'Rosh** [decisions of the Rosh]. Commentaries on his Halachot were written by a number of later Talmudists. In yeshivot, this work is studied as a regular part of the daily Talmud study.

Orchot Chaim The Ha'Rosh

This work resembles the Hilchot of the **Rif** [Rabbi Itzhak Alfasi] also an adumbration but differs in quoting later authorities - Maimonides, the Tosafists and Alfasi himself. One theory states that the work is actually not a commentary on the Talmud but is rather a commentary on the Rif, given that it always starts with the text of the **Rif**. Some however dispute this.

Rabbenu Asher's work has been printed with almost every edition of the Talmud since its publication. This work was so important in Jewish law that Yosef Karo included the Rosh together with Maimonides and Itzhak Alfasi as one of the three major **poskim** [decisors] considered in determining the final ruling in his **Shulchan Arukh**.

Rabbenu Asher's wrote - **Orchot Chaim**, an essay on ethics, written for his sons. It

Orchot Chaim The Ha'Rosh
begins with the comment - Distance yourself from haughtiness, with the essence of distancing. **Orchot Chaim** is today an important work of musar literature.

A commentary on **Zeraim** [the first order of the Mishnah] - with the exception of Tractate Berachot.

A commentary on **Tohorot** [the sixth order of the Mishnah].

The Tosefot ha-Rosh, Tosafot-like glosses on the Talmud.

A volume of responsa; see History of Responsa - Fourteenth century.

There is a volume of responsa entitled **Besamim Rosh** which is falsely attributed to the Rosh. In fact, it has been shown to

Orchot Chaim *The Ha'Rosh*

be a forgery from the 18th century, and contains controversial decisions which contradict what the Rosh wrote in his [genuine] responsa. This collection was published by Saul Berlin, Tzvi Hirsch Levin's son. It was exposed as a forgery by Mordecai Benet [amongst others]

A commentary on the Torah which often uses mystical interpretations such as using gematria and acronyms similar to his son Yaakov ben Asher more famous work Rimzei Ba'al ha-Turim.

Orchot Chaim

Chapter 1 - for Sunday

1. Avoid disagreements which are not for the sake of Heaven. Distance yourself, as much as possible, from conceit.

2. Flattering others.

3. Hypocrisy, lies, fraud and dishonesty.

4. Mockery.

5. Slandering, tale bearing, provoking others into argument.

6. And anger.

7-8. Beware of the danger in making vows. Do not deceive other people, neither in words nor in monetary matters. Do not be envious or hateful of others.

Orchot Chaim — Chapter 1

9. Never call anyone by a nickname, whether invented by you or already in existence, unless it is of a respectable nature.

10. Do not tell defamatory tales about other people, nor listen to or even believe the veracity of gossip.

11. Do not associate with loiterers and loafers, nor frequent the synagogues of the ignorant masses.

12. Do not look at a woman whom you are forbidden to marry.

13. Do not speak when handling a Cup of Blessing, such as one used during the Grace after Meals [Birkas Hamazon], until you drink from it.

Orchot Chaim — Chapter 1

14. Do not talk between **Boruch She'omar** and the end of the silent, **Shemoneh Esrei** Prayer, and including Tachanun, nor when the Chazan is reciting his Repetition, unless it is a matter of Torah, determining a Halacha or performing a pressing Mitzvah, or to greet someone with or respond to Shalom.

15. Do not talk neither when Hallel is recited nor when the Torah is being read in public.

16. Do not eat Gentile-baked bread, even from their commercial bakeries, unless Jewish-baked bread is unavailable.

17. Do not participate in dinner parties [attended by a lot of people], except if it involves a Mitzvah.

Orchot Chaim — Chapter 1

18. Do not engage in idle talk, even of those matters which there is no sin. Make it your habit to fall asleep at night whilst learning Torah, and not in the middle of a pointless conversation. That is, tire yourself on Torah.

19. Do not put yourself into a matter of doubt regarding the time of sunset and the start of Shabbos. Instruct and caution your family regarding the proper observances of Shabbos. Daven Mincha on Erev Shabbos early in order to accept the Sabbath while it is still daytime.

20. When it comes time for any of the three daily Prayers, set aside your business and pray. Concentrate on your prayers. Importantly, do not look at things which are not yours, so that you will not come to illicitly desire them.

Orchot Chaim — Chapter 1

21. Do not speak between the Washing of the Hands and the Blessing on Bread. Be first in wishing people Shalom, good morning and other such salutations.

22. Praise God for satiating your appetite and quenching your thirst. If people curse or shame you, do not answer them at all. Rather, be of those who are offended and not of those who offend. Ignore their bad behavior.

23. Do not hurry and be argumentative. Stay clear of making oaths and vows. Because of the sin of broken promises, one's young children die.

24. Distance yourself from jesting and anger, for these things confuse the minds and spirits of men. At all times serve your Creator out of love. Forget not any of these matters.

Orchot Chaim

25. Love God with all your heart and soul, and with all your resources. When you recite the Shema, sincerely intend that, were it to be necessary, you would sacrifice your life and all your assets in order to sanctify His Name; and never do anything to desecrate His Name or degrade His Commandments. By doing this, you fulfill the words of the Singer - Because[1] for your sake we are killed all the time

26. Trust God with all your heart and believe in His personal Providence; He, alone, can help everyone with everyone's needs. With this, you unify Him completely, for His Eyes rove everywhere on Earth and see all the doings of Man, without exception. He knows the hearts and minds of everyone. The one who does not believe that He "took you out of the

---

[1] Psalms 44:23

Land of Egypt" does not believe the beginning of the verse "I am the Lord, Your God", and he cannot fully make God One. What makes Israel special among the Nations of the World, and is the foundation of the entire Torah, is to make God One. This has always been at the center of the faith of Israel.

Orchot Chaim   Chapter 1

Orchot Chaim

Chapter 2 - for Monday

27. Distance yourself from arrogance and anger. Rebuke your Evil Inclination and thoughts which exhort you to listen to your own will. Do not follow them. Rather, fulfill the Will and Ways of God as revealed in the Torah, which are clear, pure and straight.

28. Distance yourself from falsehood and matters of lies. Do not use God's Name in vain nor ever express any of God's various Names in a filthy place, even if you have reason to use one of them.

29. Remove the yoke of envy which burdens the hearts of men. Rely not on people; be modest and humble before your Creator. Trust not in gold and wealth, for this is the first step in idolatry, and causes you to divert your attention from the Holy One, blessed be He. Disburse your monies as He wishes, for He has the power to restore all your losses, and satisfy all your and your household's needs.

30. Know who is this God of your fathers. Know that your words will be weighed in the Scale of Justice, and justice will be meted out. Say nothing wrong or irrational or inappropriate. Keep your word and do not change what you have promised. Make the dispersion of your monies easier than your speech. Do not be quick in speaking evil. Therefore, do not say a harsh word, even if there is good reason to nor say nothing until you weigh your words sensibly and carefully.

31. Confess your sins each morning and evening. Remember Zion and Jerusalem

Orchot Chaim — Chapter 2

with a broken heart, sincere concern, groans and tears.

32. Always have in mind the day of your demise, and equip yourself with the provisions for your final trip, that is Torah and good deeds. If you remember this at all times, as well as regretting your sins and doing repentance, you will be prepared for the day of death and your journey to the Next World; and your bed should be soaked in tears remembering your sins. It should frighten you to contemplate that even the great and pious Talmudic Scholar, Rabbi Yochanan ben Zakai of blessed memory, who was the leader of Israel during the time of the destruction of the Second Temple, and who had many outstanding students who he taught until they, themselves, were great Torah scholars, was himself afraid of his ultimate fate when he took ill. He was an exemplary

Orchot Chaim — Chapter 2

human being and learned much Torah and did enormous good. And yet, he was terrified that maybe he failed to do enough good or that possibly he may have once committed some minor injustice and, for that, Gehinna was awaiting him. All the more so should we be horrified.

33. Be a good friend to the God-fearing. Associate and bond with them. Distance yourself from those who are ungodly, lawless and unjust. Love your reprovers and their admonitions.

34. It is beneficial and proper for you to belittle your good deeds in your own eyes, while exaggerating the number and gravity of your offenses. Contemplate, at all times, the boundless compassion and unlimited grace your Creator bestows upon you; the One who feeds you when you need to be fed. Do not serve Him for recompense,

Orchot Chaim   Chapter 2

rather do so because you were so commanded, and for the glorification of His Holy Name.

35. Remember and speak of this at all times: at night when you retire, envelop yourself with love for Him. In the day, when you arise, when you go about your business, turn to Him, be quick and meticulous with your service to Him. With this, He will give you strength and support, and direct you to do His Will.

36. Pray with devotion, for prayer is worship of the heart. Think. Was your son to speak frivolously with you, would you not be angry with him? So, too, you who came from a putrid drop, standing before the King and Master of the world, should you not be earnest in your prayers? Do not be like a slave who was assigned an honorable task, one beneficial for him, and yet he spoils it. How dare he stand before the king! What, then, would be better than to ask for forgiveness when we say, **Selach lonu** (forgive us) in the Shemoneh Esrei, but worse than to recite it without conviction? If it is impossible to maintain concentration and devotion during the entire Prayer, say at least the first Blessing of the **Shemoneh Esrei** with sincerity, as well as the first verse of **Krias Shema**. For one does not fulfill his obligation for Prayer if he does not say at least these sections with intent.

37. Learn the weekly Torah portion each week, reciting the Torah text twice, the Targum once, and then learn Rashi's commentary. This should be completed before the time the Reader concludes the weekly, public Torah reading in Synagogue on Shabbos morning. Understand what Rashi is saying. Greatly

Orchot Chaim   Chapter 2

embrace and attach yourself to his commentary. When learning Talmud, be certain that you correctly understand that, too, and cling to it. For it is a proper thing to learn Mishna and Talmud, and one will receive reward for so doing. The one who sacrifices himself and carefully and scrupulously learns Talmud so that he understands it correctly, makes himself beloved. There is no greater and unique a reward than there will be for learning Torah, and no better profession than to learn Talmud. The Mishna says that learning Torah is equal, for God, to all the best Good Deeds. It is impossible to properly understand the Torah without the Talmud. Talmud Torah is equal to all else.

Orchot Chaim — Chapter 2

Orchot Chaim

Chapter 3 - for Tuesday

38. Never eat or drink anything without making the appropriate blessings before and after with as much zeal as you can. Comprehend the meaning of the blessing. Cover your head when mentioning God's Name, and close your eyes. When making a blessing or praying to God be not as it says - With[1] their mouths and lips they honored Me, but their hearts were distant from Me.

39. Wash your hands before praying and eating. When you come from the bathroom, make the **Asher Yotzar** blessing, but do not make the blessing on washing the hands.

---

[1] Isaiah 29:13

Orchot Chaim — Chapter 3

40. Make **Tzitzis** [fringes] on the four corners of your garment in order that you remember God's commandments, and in order that you sanctify yourself in all your doings. Act with modesty in the bathroom. When at home, remember that you will be held accountable for even light conversations between husband and wife. Do not accustom yourself to act frivolously, and put the fear of Heaven upon yourself. Do not gaze at a woman, even one who is unmarried. Place Mezuzahs on all your doorposts.

41. Do not reveal the secrets of others. Even non-confidential matters, keep in the confines of your heart. If you again hear these same things from someone else, do not tell him that you have heard this before. You need not tell your wife everything, and do not assume that she will keep secrets.

Orchot Chaim   Chapter 3

42. Be heedful to pray at set times in the morning, afternoon and evening. Prepare yourself an hour before the time so that you can pray with intent. Be punctual, and be of the first ten in the Minyan. Do not speak idle talk in Shul. Make sure you are not without Tallis and Tefillin.

43. Weigh carefully each step you take. Be moderate with food and drink, and with all your attributes. Take the middle path and do not veer neither to the right or left. Stick to the truth. Deal honestly with people. Vigorously pursue peace and friendship between people.

44. Establish times for Torah before you eat and before you retire to bed at night. Speak Torah at your table. Instruct the members of your household to do right; train and caution them in accordance with the ways of the Torah. Let them not speak conceitedly. Warn them against speaking in a degrading and shameful manner. Remember, the first thing a person will be judged on when he arrives before the Heavenly Court is whether or not he established times for Torah.

45. Be as happy when you are rebuked as you would be if you found great spoils of war - for which you never have to pay. The wise man loves the one who admonishes him, for open reproof is better than concealed love, and it is pleasant for him.

46. Understand how things will end up before you begin them. Contemplate the loss of not performing a Mitzvah versus the reward for performing it, as well as the punishment for sinning against the reward for avoiding the sin. The wise man sees the consequences of his actions.

Orchot Chaim — Chapter 3

47. Do not rely on your own will and judgment. Listen to advice and accept reproof. Be quick to perform your tasks, and all God's commandments. Above all, never think evil.

48. Do not accustom yourself to arise from your bed lazy. Rather, rise promptly in order to serve your Maker.

49. Run to the House of Prayer; never be late. Watch that you do not step into filth. Concentrate on your prayers and not on other matters. Be prompt to bless and glorify your Maker.

50. Do not speak mockingly or otherwise when the Chazan is praying. Be meticulous in answering Amen. Do not pray with soiled and impure hands or an unclean body, for your prayers will not be heard or accepted. Do not pray quickly nor

Orchot Chaim — Chapter 3

swallow your words. Rather, have proper intent, and pray at ease, understand what you are saying, enunciating and slightly vocalizing each word.

51. Never forget that death can come suddenly and that there will be judgment before God. Do not forget your omnipotent Creator. Direct your entire will and hopes to Him. Imagine that He is standing before you at all times.

52. Do not perform any Mitzvah in order to receive a reward nor distance yourself from sin simply to avoid punishment from Him. Rather, serve God out of true love.

Orchot Chaim

Chapter 4 - for Wednesday

53. Do not procrastinate in performing a Mitzvah which falls in your lap. Do it right away and for the sake of Heaven.

54. Do not be lazy in reciting the Blessing of the Moon, as this is a most delightful prayer for Heaven. From the time of the Exodus from Egypt until the destruction of the Temple, God dwelt amongst us in the Tabernacle and Temple, and was close to us. This is what is called the **Shechina** [God's neighboring Presence]. Now, when we sanctify the New Moon, God again draws His **Shechina** near to us. How can we not be diligent and careful that we do not omit this blessing? For if Israel did not merit anything other than receiving the **Shechina** but once a month with this prayer, this would be enough.

Orchot Chaim — Chapter 4

55. Do nothing to mislead people or that would cause them to joke about. For it is the manner of the ignorant masses to latch onto the mistakes and the bad things people do, yet they disregard the good in people.

56. Never make fun of your father or mother nor minimize their honor, and do not cause them any pain or distress. Honor them as much as you can while they are alive.

57. Do not be irate with wayfarers and your guests. Receive them with a cheerful face.

58. Do not fail to give them provisions for their journeys. Accompany them on their way, and comfort them for they are far from home and dejected.

Orchot Chaim — Chapter 4

59. Do not look towards those who are wealthier than you. Rather, turn your sights to those less fortunate than you. By so doing, you will avoid jealousy and you will be happy with your own lot, and you will be able to conduct a God-fearing and Jewish life.

60. Do not be quick to anger about anything. Be slow to anger lest you lose your wisdom.

61. Do not speak perversely and with foul language for you will be judged for all what you say. Never raise a hand against your fellow man, even were he to curse your mother or father to your face.

62. Do not remain angry with your fellow man for even one day. Beg forgiveness from him before he comes and asks forgiveness from you.

Orchot Chaim — Chapter 4

63. Do not speak conceitedly and do not be brazen so as not to accept upon yourself the fear of Heaven.

64. Do not respond to those who curse or revile you or those who call you a liar. Seal your lips and be silent lest you heat up your heart to anger.

65. Do not involve yourself in other people's disputes and don't take sides, for in the end they will reconcile and the side you took up against will be angry with you because you interfered in the argument.

66. Do not be arrogant with people. Be of a lowly spirit, and consider yourself like the dirt upon which everyone tramples.

67. Do not shame anyone or anything, for there is no one who does not have his hour

Orchot Chaim — Chapter 4

or anything which doesn't have its place or a circumstance where it is needed.

68. Pursue justice! For the one who pursues justice and righteousness and gives charity and is quick with his compassion – in words and deeds - will find life and justice and honor. Do not fail to give the half Shekel once a year. Each week and month donate as much as you can to charity. Each day, before Prayers, give at least something, however small, to charity. When you can, tithe your assets and profits. Make sure you always are stocked with food and other provisions and resources at home with which you can readily help the needy, whether they are dead or alive, poor or rich.

69. Do the Will of your Maker! Commit in your heart to discharge all what your Creator and Master has requested of you!

Orchot Chaim — Chapter 4

Be as equally happy with your portion in life whether you have been allotted a little or much. Beseech God, at all times, that He turn your heart to executing His commandments. Cast your fate with God in all what you do. Do not be stingy with regard to expenditures for all the needs of the Sabbath or the Holidays. Try and bring these days in early, while it is still daylight, for this is honor for them. Enjoy them with good food and drink, and respectful clothing, and spend half the day in the Study Hall and the synagogue. Honor these days when they begin and when they end. Set a table at the end of the Sabbath, do not sleep a lot like a indolent person. Train yourself to rise early, at sunrise. Arise from your bed at the morning chirp of the birds in order to serve the Holy One, blessed be He.

70. Do not pray with soiled and impure

Orchot Chaim   Chapter 4

hands or an unclean body, for your prayers will not be heard or accepted.

71. Do not pray quickly nor swallow your words. Rather, have proper intent, and pray at ease, understand what you are saying, enunciating and slightly vocalizing each word.

72. Do not forget your omnipotent Creator. Direct your entire will and hopes to Him. Imagine that He is standing before you at all times.

73. You ignored the Rock Who gave birth to you, and forgot God who brought you forth. In all your ways acknowledge Him, And He will make your paths smooth.

Orchot Chaim   Chapter 4

Orchot Chaim

Chapter 5 - for Thursday

74. Do not be overly joyous. Remember that life is fleeting. You are descendant of Adam, the first man, who was created from dust, and in the end, you will be consumed by worms.

75. Do not say regarding any Mitzva - **I will do it tomorrow** lest you not have the time or opportunity to do so then.

76. Do not separate yourself from learning Torah wisdom and ethics. Allow yourself to be covered with the dust of the feet of the Sages by following in their footsteps, and you, too, will become wise.

77. Never stop performing acts of loving-kindness even though others mock you for

Orchot Chaim — Chapter 5

this. Never be ashamed to perform a Mitzvah.

78. Do not clench tight your fist and desist from always giving to the poor and indigent. Never turn from helping your relatives making like you don't know them.

79. Rush to prepare food for them immediately, they may be ravenous.

80. Do not tarry in bringing a tithe to the communal kitchen. The act of bringing charity in secret checks God's anger against you.

81. Do not look up to those who are lesser than you in their Service of God or their Awe of Heaven. Rather, set your eyes on those who are greater than you in these affairs.

Orchot Chaim — Chapter 5

82. Never raise a hand against your fellow man, even were he to curse your mother or father to your face.

83. Never speak evil or slanderously about anyone. Never be contentious or spread lies about other people.

84. Do not overreact and respond hastily and vehemently to someone who speaks bad things.

85. Do not scream and yell like a wild, boorish person, for by so doing you will lose your Fear of Heaven. Do not speak so loudly at home that your voice can be heard outside of your house. Do not bellow like an animal. Always speak gently.

86. Never humiliate anyone in public for one who does so has no portion in the World to Come.

Orchot Chaim — Chapter 5

87. Never bully anyone because you are stronger than him. Remember, there may come a time when you will be the weak one.

88. Never pursue honor or authority. Never aspire to heights beyond your capabilities.

89. Never compel people to honor you because of your wealth or powerful position. Someone might resent this and will try to disgrace you or cause your downfall in return.

90. Never let up in your pursuit of making new friends and supporters. Do not take lightly even one enemy.

91. Do not consider lightly something your friend acquired, for this will upset him and cause him consternation. To do so is the manner of fools.

Orchot Chaim — Chapter 5

92. Never say - God has made me rich because of my righteousness. Rather, be worried that you have received your reward in this World, and not in the World to Come.

93. Do not cause your fellow man to turn from the good way to a bad one, like those who entice and seduce people from the worship of God.

94. Do not be a gourmand and stuff your belly with food, for many illnesses result from overeating.

95. Do not socialize with people who devour wine or are gluttonous carnivores lest you forget your Maker and make yourself ill or become sinful.

96. Do not terrorize your family and household for many serious failings result

Orchot Chaim — Chapter 5

from such behavior.

97. Never be alone in a room with any woman other than your wife, mother or daughter, and even if there are two women with you. Never look at women or their clothing.

98. Never praise a woman for her beauty or her good deeds lest others suspect her of immorality.

99. Do not venerate yourself nor make yourself precious in your own eyes. Rather, underrate yourself.

100. Act patiently. Do your work with forethought and not hastily.

101. Even regarding matters which are beneficial and not damaging, talk succinctly. Speak to the point.

Orchot Chaim — Chapter 5

102. Perpetually make efforts to acquire and maintain a faithful friend. Good friends are most beneficial.

Orchot Chaim — Chapter 5

Chapter 6 - for Friday

103. Do not inveigle your fellow man with flattery. Never say anything you do not mean.

104. Never anger a Gentile, for every Gentile has his hour; his memory is long, and he keeps his anger forever.

105. Never join with an evil person or one who is sinful or one who is angry or irate or a fool. For one day you will be shamed by them.

106. Do not even think that you can best a wise Torah scholar. You will not get any cleverer for trying to do so, nor will this result in your being considered a greater scholar.

Orchot Chaim

107. Do not be pedantic and petty with other people about every little thing they do. Doing so will result in accruing needless enemies.

108. Make no effort to learn about other people's secrets or things which have been hidden from you.

109. Do nothing in private for which you would be humiliated if done in public. Never ask, who sees me.

110. Think no evil of the one who comes to apologize to you, regardless if he is telling the truth or lying.

111. Never rely on receiving other people's gifts, for they are only human beings. Work for your sustenance.

112. Never make your money more

important for yourself than your general well-being as, for example, by putting yourself in danger by cheating on your taxes or traveling clandestinely alone.

113. Never be envious. This is a terrible, incurable illness.

114. Do not make vowing a habit, even for a true matter, for children die because of false oaths.

115. Do not be accustomed to swearing by your life, even for a true matter.

116. Never delay in making total repentance nor tarry in seeking emotional, spiritual or religious help.

117. Do not occupy yourself with useless activities. Listen not to nonsense.

Orchot Chaim — Chapter 6

118. Never call anyone by a derogatory or offensive nickname; and don't invent one for someone. For the one who does so has no place in the World to Come.

119. Do not trust in your own wealth, for anyone who trusts in his money accumulates enemies, and will falter and collapse because of them.

120. Do not make it a habit to oppose your neighbors or fellow citizens and communal leaders. Sublimate your will to theirs.

121. Do not make it a habit to eat out of your home with large groups of people other than for purposes of a Mitzvah.

122. Do not become accustomed to getting drunk. You might act foolishly or speak foul-mouthed, and then regret what you

Orchot Chaim — Chapter 6

have done.

123. Never be angry with your wife. If you pushed her away with your left hand, draw her near energetically with your right, and without delay

124. Never humiliate your wife. Rather, honor her and, by so doing, she will avoid sin.

125. Do not make it your habit to hang around with mockers and lowlifes lest they draw you into sin.

126. Do not be lazy in pursuing wisdom nor slow in respectfully rebuking your friend in private

127. Speak only when the time is right and never say anything which has no benefit. Simply, scrupulously watch what you say.

Orchot Chaim — Chapter 6

128. Never join with an evil person or one who is sinful or one who is angry or irate or a fool. For one day you will be shamed by them.

129. Do not be oblivious to the good that others do for you. Acknowledge even those who do something as simple as opening a door for you, which you surely could have done on your own.

130. Never utter a lie or speak deceitfully. Be trustworthy with everyone, Jew and Gentile alike.

131. Make an effort to be first in the saying of Shalom to everyone, Jew and Gentile alike, because of Peace.

132. Do not be accustomed to stand, for if with a wise man, hear and hear his words.

Orchot Chaim

Chapter 7 - for Saturday

Summary

1. Tithe for the benefit of charity all the profits and savings God has granted you.

2. Give charity immediately, and as much as you can. Fix an amount to give at the end of every month and year.

3. Pray three times each day, every evening, morning and afternoon with the congregation.

4. Don Tefillin and wear **Tzitzis** every day.

5. Affix a Mezuzah on every one of your doorposts and gates upon which the Law requires one. It is insufficient to have a

Orchot Chaim   Chapter 7

Mezuzah only on the front door or gate.

6. Establish fixed times for learning Torah.

7. Be faithful and honest in your business dealings, and in your speech.

8. Honor, as much as you can, those who learn Torah.

9. Do not hold back from reproving your fellow lest you carry the burden of the sin by your silence.

10. Judge your fellow man as innocent; always give him the benefit of the doubt.

11. Each night, before going to sleep, forgive anyone who sinned against you in words.

12. Try to make peace between husband

Orchot Chaim — Chapter 7

and wife, and between other people.

13. Caution your family regarding the proper observance of praying, ritually washing the hands, and reciting blessings on anything from which we benefit, such as before food, drink or things we smell.

14. Give charity every Friday.

15. Learn the weekly Torah portion by reading the text twice, the Targum once, and Rashi's commentary.

16. Read **Rabbeinu Yona's** Letter of Repentance the week before Rosh Hashanna.

17. Establish the eating of the Third Meal every Shabbos afternoon after Mincha.

18. Honor Shabbos, as it is a blessing

Orchot Chaim — Chapter 7

which your God gave to you as a present.

19. Set your table for a meal on Saturday night after Havdalah, eating at least something, however little.

20. Help your fellow man with whatever he needs, whether it is material or with words.

21. Repent every night before retiring, except on those nights when it is forbidden to deliver a eulogy or to fast. Mourn your sins, the length of the Exile, and the destruction of our glorious and holy Temple – may it be quickly rebuilt in our days.

22. Fast once each month on a day when the Torah is read. If you cannot do this, give charity.

Orchot Chaim — Chapter 7

23. Perform all your good deeds modestly and humbly, and not for public adulation. What can be done quietly should not be done with fanfare in public. For this is the Service of God which is the choicest and most desired by Him.

Orchot Chaim — Chapter 7

Orchot Chaim — Iggeret Ha'Ramban

Iggeret Ha'Ramban

Listen[1] my son to the thought of your father and do not forsake the teaching of your mother.

Accustom yourself to always speak all of your words calmly, to every man and at every time. In doing so you will prevent your anger from flaring, which is a bad attribute in a man which may cause him to sin. And accordingly said our Rabbis, may their memories be a blessing - Anyone[2] who gets angry - all of Gehinnom holds sway over him, as it says - And[3] remove the anger from your heart, and take away the bad from your flesh. and 'bad' can only

---

[1] Proverbs 1:8
[2] Nedarim 22a
[3] Kohelet 11:10

Orchot Chaim   Iggeret Ha'Ramban

mean Gehinnom, as it says - And[4] the sinner, he too, will have his day of bad.

When you will have freed yourself from anger, the quality of humility will enter your heart which is the best of all good traits, as is written - The[5] return for humility is fear of God.

Through humility you will also come to fear God. It will cause you to always think about - Where[6] you came from and where you are going," and that while alive you are only like a maggot and a worm as after death, and before Whom you will eventually stand for judgment, the Glorious King, as it is written - Even[7] the heaven and the heavens of heaven cannot

---

[4] Proverbs 16:4
[5] Mishlei 22:4
[6] Pirkei Avot 3:1
[7] Chronicles-B 6:18

Orchot Chaim

contain You - How[8] much less the hearts of people. It is also written - Do[9] I not fill heaven and earth? says the Lord.

When you think about all these things, you will come to fear God who created you, and you will protect yourself from sinning and thereby be happy with whatever happens to you. Also, when you act humbly and modestly before everyone, and fear God and sin, the radiance of His glory and the spirit of the **Shechina** [Divine Presence] will rest upon you, and you will live the life of the World to Come.

And now, my son, understand and observe that whoever feels that he is greater than others is rebelling against the Kingship of Heaven, because he is adorning himself

---

[8] Mishlei 15:11
[9] Jeremiah 23:24

Orchot Chaim — Iggeret Ha'Ramban

with His garments, as it is written - The[10] Lord reigns He wears clothes of pride.

What cause does one have for pride? Perhaps his wealth? - The[11] Lord impoverishes and enriches. Perhaps his honor? It belongs to God, as it is written - Wealth[12] and honor come from You. So how could one adorn himself with God's honor? And one who prides himself in his wisdom surely knows that God - Takes[13] away the speech of assured men and reasoning from the sages. Thus, all are equal before God, since with His anger He lowers the proud and when He wishes He raises the low. So, humble yourself and God will raise you up.

---

[10] Psalms 93:1
[11] Samuel-A 2:7
[12] Chronicles-A 29:12
[13] Job 12:20

Orchot Chaim — Iggeret Ha'Ramban

Therefore, I will now explain to you how to always behave humbly. Speak gently at all times, with your head bowed, your eyes looking down to the ground and your heart focusing on God. Don't look at the face of the person to whom you are speaking. Consider everyone as greater than yourself. If he is wise or wealthy, you should give him respect. If he is poor and you are wealthier or wiser than he, consider yourself to be more guilty than he, and that he is more worthy than you, since when he sins it is inadvertent, while you act knowingly.

In all your actions, words and thoughts, always regard yourself as standing before God, with His **Shechinah** [Divine Presence] above you, for His glory fills the whole world. Speak with fear and awe, as a servant in the presence of his master.

Orchot Chaim — Iggeret Ha'Ramban

Act with restraint in front of everyone. When someone calls you, don't answer loudly, but calmly, as one who stands before his master.

Take heed to study Torah constantly, so you will be able to fulfill its commands. When you arise from your learning reflect carefully on what you have studied, to find a lesson in it that you can be put into practice. Examine your actions every morning and evening, and in this way every one of your days will be spent in returning to God.

Remove all worldly concerns from your heart during prayer. Prepare your heart before God, purify your thoughts and think about the words before you utter them.

Do this each and every day of your life, in all of your activities and you will not come

Orchot Chaim — Iggeret Ha'Ramban

to sin. This way all your words, deeds and thoughts will be proper, your prayers will be pure, clear, clean, appropriate and acceptable to God, as it is written - When[14] their heart is directed to You, listen to them.

Read this letter at least once a week and not less. Fulfill it, and in so doing, walk with it forever in the ways of the Lord, may He be blessed, so that you will succeed in all your ways. This is how you will succeed and merit the World to Come which is reserved for the righteous. Every day that you shall read this letter, heaven shall answer whatever arises in your heart to request, forever. Amen, Sela.

---

[14] Psalms 10:17

Orchot Chaim　　Iggeret Ha'Ramban

Orchot Chaim

Iggeret Ha'Gra

I ask you to refrain from becoming sad, as you truly promised me, and not to worry - [**Another wording:** as Mother promised me - besides, what is there to worry about]? It is common for men to leave their wives in order to travel and wander destitute for years to make money. But I, thank God, am traveling to the Holy Land - which everyone longs to see - The[1] Jewish people's Most Beloved [**Another wording:** Hashem's Most Beloved, desired by all heavenly and earthly beings]. And I am traveling in peace, thank God. You are also aware that I have left behind my children, for whom my heart moans, and all my precious books - And[2] I am as a stranger in a foreign

---

[1] Samuel-A 9:20
[2] Jeremiah 14:8

Orchot Chaim — Iggeret Ha'Gra

country. Yes, I have left everything behind, etc.

It is well-known that this world is all emptiness, that every amusement is worthless, and woe is anyone who pursues vanity, which is worthless. And don't envy the rich, for - Here[3] is a grave evil I have observed under the sun riches hoarded by their owner to his misfortune. In[4] that those riches are lost in some unlucky venture and if he begets a son he has nothing in hand. Another[5] grave evil is this He must depart just as he came as he came out of his mother's womb so must he depart at last naked as he came. He can take nothing of his wealth to carry with him. So[6] what

---

[3] Koheles 5:12
[4] Koheles 5:13
[5] Koheles 5:14
[6] Koheles 5:15

Orchot Chaim   Iggeret Ha'Gra

is the good of his toiling for the wind. Yes[7] even if the other lived a thousand years twice over but never had his fill of enjoyment for are not both of them bound for the same place. Even[8] if a man lives many years let him enjoy himself in all of them remembering how many the days of darkness are going to be the only future is nothingness. Of[9] revelry I said it's mad of merriment What good is that. Tomorrow you will cry for having laughed today. Do not lust after imaginary honor, for it is worthless and time is a trait Another wording: it is like scales, which lift the light and lower the weighty. The world is like one who drinks salty water - He thinks it quenches his thirst, but it only makes him thirstier. It is said in the Midrash - No[10]

---

[7] Koheles 6:6
[8] Koheles 11:8
[9] Koheles 2:2
[10] Koheles Rabbah 1

Orchot Chaim   Iggeret Ha'Gra

one leaves the world with even half his cravings fulfilled. What[11] profit does one have from all his toils under the sun.

Enjoy[12] happiness with a woman you love all the fleeting days of life that have been granted to you under the sun all your fleeting days for that alone is what you can get out of life and out of the means you acquire under the sun.], but who are being judged severely for them. And of what benefit is gratification to man - whose end is dust, maggots and worms, as he is bound to die - when all his enjoyments turn to bitterness in the grave? And what is this world, whose days are full of anguish and pain which prevent one from sleeping? Neither is death a mikveh. Man will be judged for everything he says; even the slightest expression is not overlooked.

---

[11] Koheles 1:3
[12] Koheles 9:6

Orchot Chaim — Iggeret Ha'Gra

Therefore, I exhort you to train yourself to sit as much as possible, because the sin of the tongue is the most severe, as our Sages said - These[13] are the things...and lashon hara is equivalent to them all. I don't have to elaborate on this most serious sin of all. All[14] man's toil is for his mouth. Our Sages said that all man's mitzvas and teachings are not enough to counterbalance what comes out of his mouth. What[15] should be a man's pursuit in this world? He should be silent. One must seal his lips as tight as two millstones. Idle words are like powerful weapons which can reach from one end of the world to the other. Now, this is true concerning mere excessive speech. Where forbidden speech is concerned - e.g. lashon hara, mocking, swearing, vowing, fighting and cursing - especially in the synagogue,

---

[13] Tosefta Pe'ah 1
[14] Koheles 6:7
[15] Chullin 89a

Orchot Chaim — Iggeret Ha'Gra

and on Shabbos and Yom Tov - for every utterance of this type it is impossible to imagine the pain and suffering one will receive Zohar! No word is lost; everything is recorded. Winged beings attach themselves to everyone, recording all they say. For[16] a bird of the skies may carry the sound, and some winged creature may tell the matter. Let[17] not your mouth cause your flesh to sin and do not tell the messenger that it was an error. Why should God be angered by your speech and destroy the work of your hands. Purchase all your needs through a messenger, even if this would cost two or three times as much. Is[18] there a limit to what God can provide. Hashem[19] feeds all creatures, from the greatest to the smallest, and provides all

---

[16] Koheles 10:20
[17] Koheles 5:5
[18] Bamidbar 11:23
[19] Avodah Zarah

Orchot Chaim   Iggeret Ha'Gra

their needs.

And on Shabbos and Yom Tov do not speak at all about things that are not urgent, and be brief even with what is important, for the Shabbos is very holy. And[20] our Sages barely permitted the exchange of greetings on it. See how strict they were concerning even a single expression! Continue to give great honor to the Shabbos as when I was there. Do not cut back on your Shabbos expenses, since - Man's[21] entire sustenance [for the year is fixed for him from Rosh Hashana to Yom Kippur, except the expenditure for Sabbaths and Festivals, etc.

I also implore and plead with you to guide your daughters very carefully to refrain from cursing, swearing, lying and fighting.

---

[20] Shabbat 113:1
[21] Beitzah 16a

Orchot Chaim — Iggeret Ha'Gra

Rather, everything they do should be done peacefully, with love, affection and gentleness. I have left behind several Yiddish books on **Mussar** [morality]. See that the children read them constantly, especially on the Holy Shabbos, when **Mussar** is the only thing, they should read. Always instruct them according to **Mussar** books. Don't hold back from hitting them when they curse, swear or lie. Don't be lenient with them, because parents will be punished severely for the corruption of their children, God forbid. And even if one constantly teaches them **Mussar**, but they do not follow it, one's sorrow and shame in the World-to-Come will be great. As it is written in the Midrash - She[22] defiles her father - in such a case the son of a righteous man is called - The[23] son of a wicked man. Similarly, in other

---

[22] Vayikra 21:9
[23] Sanhedrin 52a

Orchot Chaim — Iggeret Ha'Gra

matters, lashon hara and gossip. Their eating and drinking should always be preceded and followed by the appropriate blessings. They must be careful to say the blessings, **Birkas Hamazon** [grace after meals], and **Krias Shema** [Shema reading] with proper **kavanah** [intent]. Most importantly, they must not wander outside the home and must obey and respect you and my mother and all their elders. They also need to observe all that is written in the **Mussar** books.

Raise your own children as well correctly and sensitively, and pay their tutor well, for - Man's[24] entire sustenance for the year is fixed for him from Rosh Hashanah...except **Ti'Sh'Re'Y'** [initials of - **T**almud Torah, **S**habbos, **R**osh Chodesh and **Y**om Tov].

---

[24] Beitzah 16a

Orchot Chaim — Iggeret Ha'Gra

I have also left books for them. For Hashem's sake, guide them well and gently. Take care of their health and make sure that they always have enough to eat. First have them learn the entire Chumash, seeing to it that they know it almost by heart. The learning must be done without undue pressure, rather gently, because it is best absorbed when one is relaxed. Give them coins, etc., as a reward.

Always focus your attention on these matters and not on others, because all else is trivial. For[25] man can salvage nothing from his labor to take with him. See except two white garments shrouds. Also - Ah[26] it cannot redeem a man or pay his ransom to God. Do[27] not be afraid when a man becomes rich when his household goods

---

[25] Koheles 5:14
[26] Tehillim 49:8
[27] Tehillim 49:17

Orchot Chaim   Iggeret Ha'Gra

increase. For[28] when he dies he can take none of it along his goods cannot follow him down. Don't say - I[29] will leave a portion for my children who will tell you in the grave The children of man are like grasses of the field, some blossom and some fade. Everyone is born under his constellation and Divine Providence. They are glad when he dies and he goes into the nether world. At his death Resh Lakish left his children a **kav** [The weight 24 eggs] of saffron, and he applied to himself the verse - For[30] one sees that the wise die that the foolish and ignorant both perish leaving their wealth to others. Woe[31] to all who plan on leaving wealth to their children. The only reward from sons and daughters is through their Torah and good deeds.

---

[28] Tehillim 49:18
[29] Eruvin 54a
[30] Tehillim 49:11
[31] Gittin 47a

Orchot Chaim — Iggeret Ha'Gra

Their[32] sustenance is fixed for them. It is also known that women earn merit by making their children learn Torah etc.

Our Sages said in the Midrash - The[33] only proper wife is one that does her husband's will. Of course, I am writing you words of the Living God. Therefore, I am certain that you will follow all that I have written. Nevertheless, I wish to strongly advise you not to deviate from anything that I have written. Read this letter every week, especially on Shabbos before and during the meal, in order to prevent idle talk and, even worse, lashon hara and the like, God forbid.

I reiterate my request that you guide your sons and daughters with words of kindness and **Mussar** that will find a place in their

---

[32] Berachos 17a
[33] Tanna D'Vei Eliyahu Rabba 9

Orchot Chaim — Iggeret Ha'Gra

heart. This is true especially if we merit to arrive in Eretz Yisrael, because one must be extra cautious to follow Hashem's ways there. Therefore, train them well, since one must work hard on one's speech and character traits. And[34] only through good habits can we control ourselves. All[35] beginnings are hard. But[36] afterwards one is worthy of praise. For the wicked person knows that he is taking the wrong path, but it is hard for him to change. But this is man's main task, not to go after his desires, but - To[37] restrain himself with a bit and bridle when he is being groomed. Man must deprive himself until he dies, not by fasting or asceticism, but by controlling his mouth and desires. This is teshuvah. And this is the whole reward of the World-

---

[34] Shaarey Teshuvah
[35] Mechilta Yisro
[36] Mishlei 20:14
[37] Tehillim 32:9

Orchot Chaim — Iggeret Ha'Gra

to-Come, as it is written - For[38] the commandment is a lamp and the Torah is a light. - but [The continuation of the verse is] - The way to life is the rebuke that disciplines. And that is worth more than any amount of fasting and self-affliction. For[39] every second that man controls his tongue, he merits some of the **Hidden** by Hashem for the righteous light, something which no angel or other creature can imagine. And it is stated - Who[40] is the man who is eager for life who desires years of good fortune. Guard[41] your tongue from evil your lips from deceitful speech. This will atone for any sin and save one from **Gehinnom**, as we find - He[42] who guards his mouth, from too much eating and

---

[38] Mishlei 6:23
[39] Chofetz Chaim gate 1:11
[40] Tehillim 34:13
[41] Tehillim 34:14
[42] Mishlei 21:23

Orchot Chaim — Iggeret Ha'Gra

drinking and tongue from idle words guards himself from trouble. Also - Death[43] and life are in the power of the tongue. Woe to one who gives away his life for one word. If[44] the snake bites because no spell was uttered, no advantage is gained by the trained charmer. And - Everything has a cure except, etc. It is most important to refrain from speaking words of praise about anyone. How much more so does this apply to speaking ill of anyone! Why must one speak about others? The[45] mouth that speaks strangely is a deep pit he who angers Hashem falls into it.

Concerning solitude, the main thing is to remain at home. Even your visit to the synagogue should be very short. In fact, it

---

[43] Mishlei 18:21
[44] Koheles 10:11
[45] Mishlei 22:14

Orchot Chaim   Iggeret Ha'Gra

is better to pray at home, for it is impossible to be spared from jealousy or from hearing idle talk or lashon hara in the synagogue. And one receives punishment for this, as we find [Shabbos 33a], Even[46] one who hears vulgar speech and is silent is punished, as it is stated he that is abhorred of the Lord shall fall therein even if he himself does not speak at all. This is even the more so on Shabbos and Yom Tov when they gather to talk - It is then better that you don't pray at all. Refrain also from going to the cemetery especially women, as it leads to all kinds of sorrow and sin. It is also advisable that your daughter not go to the synagogue, because she'll see beautiful clothes there, become jealous and talk about it at home. This will lead to lashon hara, etc. She should rather cling to **Mussar** and not become jealous of

---

[46] Shabbat 33a

Orchot Chaim   Iggeret Ha'Gra

anything in this world, where everything is vanity and illusions. You[47] cared about the plant which you did not work for and which you did not grow which appeared overnight and perished overnight. Though[48] he grows as high as the sky His head reaching the clouds. He[49] perishes forever, like his dung those who saw him will say where is he. For[50] property does not last forever, or a crown for all generations. And even while it exists it is worthless, loathsome and disdained by any sensible person. Woe to him who is impressed by it. Do[51] not envy sinners in your heart but only God-fearing men at all times. She should not say - How can I earn a share in the World-to-Come I can't do it.

---

[47] Yonah 4:10
[48] Iyov 20:6
[49] Iyov 20:7
[50] Mishlei 27:24
[51] Mishlei 23:17

Orchot Chaim   Iggeret Ha'Gra

For we have learned One may do much or one may do little, provided he directs his heart to heaven.

For the sake of Hashem, give a fifth of all earnings to charity. Do not give less, as I have already warned you, because that causes the transgression of several positive and negative mitzvahs every minute! It also implies a rejection of the Holy Torah, God forbid.

But the main way to merit Olam Haba is by guarding one's tongue. That is worth more than all the Torah and good deeds. This is the meaning of - You[52] carefree women Attend, hear my words You confident ladies Give ear to my speech. Because[53] the mouth is the holiest of the holy.

---

[52] Isaiah 32:9
[53] Berachos 17a

Orchot Chaim — Iggeret Ha'Gra

Among my books is a copy of **Mishlei** with Yiddish translation. For the sake of Hashem, have them read it daily. It is better than any **Mussar** book. They should also read **Koheles** a lot because it points out the vanity of this world, and other books as well. But God forbid that reading should be the objective! Reading **Mussar** alone does not necessarily move one to act differently. Going out into the world without a good understanding of it defeats the whole purpose. It is like one sow without having plowed; the wind and birds will carry the seeds away because they aren't closed off and protected. So, is he who merely reads **Mussar** like him who plants without a fence; pigs will eat and trample on everything? Some plant on stone. This is comparable to a heart of stone which cannot be penetrated unless it is struck until it breaks open. That's why I wrote you to hit our children if they don't obey you. Train[54] a lad in the way he ought to go. This is an important principle of education.

I also wish to appeal to my son-in-law to adhere to all the above. Read to the children as I have stated and learn for the sake of Heaven. Become well-versed in it for Hashem's sake. Don't pay attention to those who say that it is unnecessary for the child, God forbid. To the contrary, "Train a lad, etc." It is easier to remove the skin of a nut before it hardens into a shell. Most importantly, it is through such study that one merits everything, as our Sages stated in the Mishna - Rabbi[55] Meir said whoever studies Torah for its own sake merits many things furthermore the whole world is worthwhile for his sake alone. You should study Tractate **Avos**, especially **Avos**

---

[54] Mishlei 22:6
[55] Avos 6:1

Orchot Chaim

Iggeret Ha'Gra

D'Rabbi Noson, and Tractate **Derech Eretz**, since **Derech Eretz** good manners are more important than Torah study. Honor both your mother-in-law and your children's great grandmother. Also always treat everyone with politeness and respect.

My Dear Mother, I know that you don't need my advice, because you are very modest. Nevertheless, I wish someone would read this letter to you, for it consists of words of the Living God. I beg of you not to grieve over me, as you promised me, and God willing, if I merit to arrive at the gate of heaven in the holy city of Jerusalem, I will pray for you as I promised. And if we deserve it, we shall all be reunited, please God. I also ask my wife to honor my mother, as the Torah dictates, especially since she is a widow to whom it is a grave sin to cause even the slightest pain. I also ask you, Mother, to please

Orchot Chaim — Iggeret Ha'Gra

cause peace to reign between you, and that you should strive to bring happiness one to the other. This is a great mitzvah incumbent upon everyone, as we find - When[56] man is judged, he will be asked, did you make your fellow a king over you? We see that one must gladly enhance his friend's honor. In fact, the main goal of the Torah is to bring joy to man. Even if one of you should happen to act improperly, excuse each other and live in peace for Hashem's name. I also ask of you, Mother, to supervise and guide my children with gentle words, so that they will accept them. I instruct my sons and daughters to honor her, and not to fight among themselves at all, but to settle everything peacefully.

May the Master of Peace grant you, my

---

[56] Reishis Chochmah

Orchot Chaim — Iggeret Ha'Gra

sons, daughters, sons-in-law, brother and all Israel life and peace.

You're loving Eliyahu the son of Rabbi Shlomo Zalman ztz"l.

Orchot Chaim — Iggeret Ha'Gra